# THE
# SMART
## STEPFAMILY
### Participant's
### Guide

**SMART**
**STEPFAMILY**
SERIES

## Books in the Smart Stepfamily Series

FROM BETHANY HOUSE PUBLISHERS

*101 Tips for the Smart Stepmom*
(Laura Petherbridge)

*Daily Encouragement for the Smart Stepfamily*
(Ron L. Deal with Dianne Neal Matthews)

*Dating and the Single Parent*
(Ron L. Deal)

*The Smart Stepdad*
(Ron L. Deal)

*The Smart Stepfamily*
(Ron L. Deal)

*The Smart Stepfamily DVD*
(Ron L. Deal)

*The Smart Stepfamily Guide to Financial Planning*
(Ron L. Deal, Greg S. Pettys, and David O. Edwards)

*The Smart Stepfamily Participant's Guide*
(Ron L. Deal)

*The Smart Stepfamily Marriage*
(Ron L. Deal and David H. Olson)

*The Smart Stepmom*
(Ron L. Deal and Laura Petherbridge)

*In Their Shoes*
(Lauren Reitsema)

FROM FAMILYLIFE PUBLISHING

*Life in a Blender* (booklet for kids)
(Ron L. Deal)

*The Smart Stepfamily Marriage Small-Group Study Guide*
(Ron L. Deal)

# THE
# SMART
# STEPFAMILY
## Participant's Guide

An **8** Session Guide
to a Healthy Stepfamily

# RON L. DEAL

BETHANYHOUSE
*a division of Baker Publishing Group*
Minneapolis, Minnesota

© 2014, 2019 by Ron L. Deal

Published by Bethany House Publishers
11400 Hampshire Avenue South
Bloomington, Minnesota 55438
www.bethanyhouse.com

Bethany House Publishers is a division of
Baker Publishing Group, Grand Rapids, Michigan

Revised edition published 2019

Printed in the United States of America

Library of Congress Cataloging-in-Publication Data for the original edition is on file at the Library of Congress, Washington, DC.

ISBN 978-0-7642-3566-5 (rev.)

Scripture quotations are from the Holy Bible, New International Reader's Version®. NIrV®. Copyright © 1995, 1996, 1998 by Biblica, Inc.™ Used by permission of Zondervan. All rights reserved worldwide. www.zondervan.com

Cover design by Eric Walljasper

19  20  21  22  23  24  25      7  6  5  4  3  2  1

# Contents

Welcome & Getting the Most From This Series   7

Session 1:  Becoming a Smart Stepfamily   13

Session 2:  STEP Up to Discover a Redemptive God   19

Session 3:  STEP Down Your Expectations   25

Session 4:  STEP Through the Wilderness Wanderings   33

Session 5:  Two-STEP: Your Marriage   39

Session 6:  Side STEP Common Pitfalls   45

Session 7:  STEP in Line With the Parenting Team   51

Session 8:  STEP Over Into the Promised Land   59


Bonus Material   65
   *Family Meetings: A Tool for Problem Solving*   66
   *Smart Questions, Smart Answers*   69
Group Leader Notes   101
My Action Plan   109

# Welcome

Family life presents many challenges; stepfamilies face additional challenges unique to them, but with God's guidance and the support of friends, facing those challenges can bring great rewards. It is my prayer that this series will help enrich your family and provide you the tools to create a healthy, Christ-centered family.

Ron L. Deal

## Getting the Most From This Series

Whether you are an individual, couple, or group of couples studying this series together, this participant's guide can be adapted for your needs. Each session walks you through discussion questions and practical advice for how to strengthen your home. Individuals and couples are welcome to complete the study by themselves (e.g., as part of a premarital counseling program), but we strongly recommend that you work through the material with a group of couples if possible (e.g., small group or Bible class). Research and my experience in stepfamily ministry suggest that fellowship and group discussion with other stepfamily couples is a vital part of applying the principles of this study. Together you will support each other and discover how to become a smart stepfamily. Pre-stepfamily couples are encouraged to attend groups with married couples to glean from their experience.

There are many different kinds of stepfamilies. Some are empty-nest with adult stepchildren and stepgrandchildren; others have young children. Some follow divorce, others the death of a spouse (or both), and others a non-marital birth. Still others have multiple homes to which children are moving back and forth, while other stepfamilies don't send children to any other home. These differences create opportunities for you as group members to learn from the perspective of others with situations different than yours and to practice empathy. Being able to hear, validate, and appreciate the experience of someone else is a very important skill for healthy stepfamilies. Practice this skill during your group discussions and take the skill home with you.

Let me make a few other recommendations for your study.

- Start your group study by agreeing to the guidelines at the end of this section. Following these will help create a safe discussion environment for everyone.

- Use this guide to take notes during the video presentation; each person should have their own participant's guide (two per couple) because experience tells me that you will take different notes depending on whether you are a parent or stepparent, male or female, an insider or outsider. It's important that each of you be allowed to process the video presentation through the lens of your family experience and role.

- Discussion questions before and after the video will help you assimilate and apply the teaching, so don't skip them. For optimum learning, groups should structure sessions to last 90 minutes so you have plenty of time to discuss and process the video content.

- To get the most from this study you should purchase a copy of my book *The Smart Stepfamily: Seven Steps to a Healthy Family, Revised and Expanded Edition*. Some sessions invite you to read portions of the book aloud and discuss them. Plus, to reinforce important concepts, each session concludes with recommended reading from the book. This is important because the book offers additional content and addresses specific types of stepfamilies (e.g., those following death or later-in-life stepfamilies) that the video does not. When experienced in combination, the video and book make an excellent learning system.

This guide, when referencing the book or recommended reading, corresponds best to the *Revised and Expanded Edition (2014)* of *The Smart Stepfamily.* You can get by with a previous edition of the book, but it is recommended that everyone in a group use the Revised and Expanded Edition so you're all reading off the same page.

- I'd also like to recommend that you go online and take the Couple Checkup as a supplemental enrichment tool (available at www.SmartStepfamilies.com). This relationship profile is the most researched inventory of its kind and will give you great insight into the strengths of your relationship. I call it your Couple Positioning System (CPS). Like a GPS device that pinpoints your current location and then provides directions to your destination, this CPS device identifies your relationship strengths and growth areas and provides specific feedback on how you can deepen trust and closeness. The inventory adapts to your couple type, whether dating, engaged, or married, and provides personal feedback for your relationship. It only takes about thirty minutes to complete the inventory. I strongly encourage you to make use of this wonderful tool.

## Additional Study

These resources can supplement this study or serve as follow-up studies for your group.

- The book *The Smart Stepfamily Marriage* (Ron L. Deal and David H. Olson) and the accompanying study guide is a recommended follow-up study to *The Smart Stepfamily DVD.* Together the two studies provide a comprehensive system for strengthening your marriage and stepfamily. This book is recommended for dating and married couples alike.

- *The Smart Stepmom* (with Laura Petherbridge) and *The Smart Stepdad* are recommended to both stepparents and biological parents (both include discussion questions for groups). Learning to work together as a parenting team is critical to the success of your marriage and family.

- *Dating and the Single Parent* is a must-read for dating or engaged couples. It will walk you through the stages of dating, help you discern what is best for the children, and once engaged equip you for life after the wedding.

- *The Smart Stepfamily Guide to Financial Planning* helps couples create a practical plan for managing money and organizing their estate while strengthening their family.

- *Daily Encouragement for the Smart Stepfamily* is a one-year devotional for blended couples that offers practical advice to keep your family on track. In under one minute each day you can take 365 steps in the right direction.

- *Life in a Blender,* a booklet for children ages 10 and up, helps children adapt to their stepfamily, and the accompanying parent discussion guide connects parents to the hearts of their children. Available at FamilyLife.com.

## Group Leaders

Guidelines for effective group discussion and instructions for leading your group through this material are available at the back of this guide.

### Group Guidelines

1. **Confidentiality**—We agree that what is said here stays here. We honor one another's privacy and will not share stories or details heard in the group meeting with people who are not in attendance.
2. **Honor**—Couples agree not to share intimate details without first asking our partner whether it is okay to share with the group. If you're not sure it's okay to share, then it probably isn't. Wait and ask your spouse outside of the group.
3. **Advice**—We agree not to offer unsolicited advice to one another. If after telling about a frustration someone receives advice, they might feel judged and pressured to abide by the advice. This creates a sharing barrier for them and others in the future. Agree to give advice only if someone first asks for the group's input.
4. **Respect**—We agree to show common courtesy to one another. Examples include allowing everyone to talk (not dominating the group discussion time), not interrupting, not engaging in side conversations during the group discussion, and showing up on time. Even making a commitment to regular attendance shows respect to others who are counting on us to be there. Call if you cannot attend a session.
5. **Acceptance and Encouragement**—We agree to build one another up in the Lord. We will share our faith, love, and support and strive to walk alongside one another in mutual encouragement. If we disagree, we will continue to love in spite of our differences.

**Session**

**1**

# Becoming a Smart Stepfamily

## OPEN

Before the video presentation discuss the following:

1. What have you been thinking or feeling as you anticipated attending this first session?
2. What is one question you hope to get answered in this series?
3. Share a brief sketch of your family, including whether you are dating or married, how many children you have, and who their parents are. Just for fun, share one humorous story or aspect about your family that most people do not know.
4. Pray for God's blessing as you begin this journey together.

**W**ATCH (take notes from the video presentation here)

Marriage and family is one of God's greates tools for growing us up.

Stepfamilies come in many shapes and sizes.

- Complexity equals _____ and stress _____ blood.

- Death, divorce, or a dissolved relationship does not _____ family life, it just reorganizes it.

## Three Takeaways

- The dream seemed simple, but reality is far more _____.

- Accept that there are people in your life you didn't

  _____.

- You need stepfamily _____ to stepfamily questions.

# **D**ISCUSS

1. Which of the two common responses to *The Smart Stepfamily* can you relate to most?

2. Children are part of the family package. How do children both bless and complicate your couple relationship? Can you remember what was happening when you first realized that your family is more complex than you had thought?

3. Have you known a stepcouple who has been married for a number of years? What positive qualities do they possess?

4. Accepting the reality of having family members you didn't choose can be difficult. Share a time this reality frustrated you. In what way has it frustrated your children?

   • When it comes to accepting difficult family members, a few biblical attitudes might help. Read Colossians 3:12–14. How might these qualities be helpful?

5. What concern has this session raised that you'd like to discuss?

6. What would you like to celebrate about your family?

## ⒶPPLY

During each session take a few minutes to reflect how you will apply what you have learned. (Sharing this decision with the group is optional.)

- How will you apply this session? Consider this your personal action plan. Later, you can transfer your key action points to the My Action Plan summary at the end of this guide for easy access and to remind you of your plans.

## ⒫RAY

Prayer Requests to Honor This Week:

- Share one aspect of your family you hope to see improved as a result of this study. (Record the prayer requests of others here.)

- Pray over your group list.

## ⓡEAD

Recommended Reading for This Week:

- *The Smart Stepfamily, Revised and Expanded,* chapter 1

Remember to bring this guide with you to each session.

Session

**2**

# STEP Up to Discover a Redemptive God

**O**PEN

Before the video:

1. In what way have you applied last week's lesson? Even if it didn't bring about the desired result, share what you tried.
2. Sometimes people in stepfamilies feel like second-class Christians because of divorce or because their families are different than biological families. In what way can you relate to that? Do you know others who may feel that way?

ATCH

STEP Up!—to discover a redemptive God who loves, forgives, and provides strength and direction for your journey.

1. Feeling unworthy

2. Biblical families: Far less than ideal
   • Jacob . . .

   • Rachel and Leah . . .

3. The "D and R" mean:

4. You're not a second-class Christian because there's no such thing as a _____ Christian.

5. Stop hiding in shame. Your shame has been _____.

# **D**ISCUSS

Discuss the following:

1. How does the survey of Old Testament families make you feel about your home?

2. To what degree have you been alienated from Christ in the past? What was happening at that time?

3. What part of your life would you change today if you didn't feel the shame of the past? If you didn't fear judgment from others?

4. Whether your relationship with Christ is just beginning or strong, list three habits that would deepen your knowledge of God's Word and help you walk with him.

How might you encourage your children to also develop these habits?

5. Do you suppose that the children (of all ages) in your family feel some shame about their family or feel like second-class citizens? What might contribute to that? How might you attend to that?

6. Embracing the grace of Christ is a big decision, and once you do, entails a life of discipleship. Share a personal victory in your walk with Christ and/or an area of your walk that needs prayer.

# PPLY

How will you apply the principles of this session? Remember to transfer key thoughts to the My Action Plan at the end of this guide.

# **P**RAY

Prayer Requests to Honor This Week:

# **R**EAD

Recommended Reading for This Week:

- *The Smart Stepfamily, Revised and Expanded,* chapter 3 (Note: You will read chapter 2 later in the study.)

Session 3

# STEP Down Your Expectations

## OPEN

Before the video:

1. After the last lesson did anyone experience greater fellowship with God or a stronger sense of hope this past week? In what way?

2. What is one expectation (e.g., related to your marriage, family, or stepparent role) that you had before the wedding that you now realize was unrealistic?

3. What do you wish you had known or understood more completely before you married?

# ATCH

Unrealistic expectations foster disappointment and discouragement.

1. How do you cook a stepfamily?

   • A common unrealistic strategy is with a blender. Examples:

2. You cook a stepfamily with a _____.

   It works on time and low heat.
   • Married couples: focus on creating warmth in the pot.

   • Dating couples: maintain sexual purity but don't rush into marriage.

   Low-heat tool #1:

Low-heat tool #2:[1]

Two opposing forces: "merging" and "staying put"

3. The average stepfamily takes _____ years to integrate.
   • But what if . . .

   • There are many Crockpot factors you can't control. What you can do is maintain low heat for an extended period of time.

4. If today is not what you want it to be, trust that the Crockpot is still cooking.

1. Patricia Papernow, *Becoming a Stepfamily*, New York: Gardner Press, 1993.

# **D**ISCUSS

1. In what ways has this lesson given you hope? In what way has it discouraged you?

2. What is going well in your home? (Acknowledge your strengths so you can build on them.)

3. Which of the following myths have you believed, maybe even pushed to make happen?

   • Love will occur instantly between all family members.
   • All children will support your marriage and long for your marital success as much as you do.
   • Blending is the goal.

4. We often behave in a way consistent with what we believe. What actions have you taken because of the myth(s) you believed? (For example, becoming angry with a child who wasn't necessarily overjoyed at your wedding announcement or withdrawing in shame for not loving your stepchildren as much as you think you should.)

5. What "blender strategies" have you tried? What has been the result of your pushing?

6. If you adopted a Crockpot mentality, what thoughts or behaviors would you start changing today?

7. Compartmentalization scares some people because it feels like they're being left out. When balanced with middle ground time, compartmentalization is an investment of time that returns more than it demands—it is a gift to everyone. How might you apply these principles in your home? Give specific examples.

8. Discuss this statement: Stepping down expectations is about accepting reality and not inadvertently setting yourself up for disappointment or adding undue "blender" pressure to other family members.

9. What advice would you give a dating couple with children about to marry?

## **A**PPLY

How will you apply these principles this coming week? Over the next few months? During the next special day or holiday?

## **P**RAY

Prayer Requests to Honor This Week:

## **R**EAD

Recommended Reading for This Week:

- *The Smart Stepfamily, Revised and Expanded,* chapter 4
- Consider doing the recommended family activity found in the parent-child discussion section at the end of chapter 4

of *The Smart Stepfamily, Revised and Expanded* before your next session.

- Pre-stepfamily couples—see the special exercise below.

## Special Exercise for Pre-Stepfamily Couples

### *"What's in a name?" Negotiating Terms for Parents and Stepparents*

As stepfamilies begin the process of bonding and forming a family identity, the names or terms you use to refer to one another can be very important. They symbolize expectations, differing levels of relational connection (e.g., "Daddy" vs. "Mom's husband"), and remind everyone that there are important people not living in your home. Negotiating these terms in a healthy way is important. As you approach the wedding, consider taking these steps:

**Step 1:** The biological parent should have a private conversation with their children about possible terms for the stepparent after the wedding (for later-life couples this includes adult children). Preface the discussion by outlining your expectations. Share your understanding that using "Dad" or "Mommy" to refer to a stepparent can create feelings of guilt when a child considers how their other biological parent will feel (or how a deceased parent might feel). Explain that they don't have to use such a term unless they want to and that you won't dictate what term they use as long as it is respectful. Also, it's okay for different children to decide to use different terms.

Ask:

1. In what way have you felt the pressure to call your future stepparent Dad or Mom?
2. How do you think your biological dad or mom would react if they heard you use a term like that?

3. What are some terms you've considered using? (Brainstorm a list.) Other children have used "stepdad," "Tom," or "bonus dad."
4. In public, how will you introduce them?
5. How do you want him/her to introduce you?

Close the meeting with your children by explaining that you will now share the list of possible terms with your future spouse (their stepparent). Then, all of you can meet to decide which is best for everyone.

**Step 2:** Meet with your fiancé to share your impressions from the meeting with your children. Set up a time for the adults and children to meet together.

**Step 3:** Have a family meeting with the stepparent present. The stepparent should begin the meeting by sharing their expectations. Here's a possible script to build from: "I want you kids to understand that I know I'm not your dad/mom. You have/had one of those already and they deserve a very special place in your heart. I'm not going to try to replace your dad/mom and I don't expect you to call me anything you don't feel comfortable with. So don't worry about hurting my feelings. We're here to make sure we all feel comfortable with how we refer to one another."

The couple should then lead the discussion:

1. Share the brainstormed terms with which you feel comfortable.
2. Ask the children which term is their preferred term when in private and which they prefer in public.
3. Negotiate the options until you can all agree on a given term.

Go out as a group for a fun activity (e.g., getting ice cream) and celebrate your decision.

# STEP Through the Wilderness Wanderings

## OPEN

Before the video:

1. Did anyone do the family activity (at the end of chapter 4 of *The Smart Stepfamily, Revised and Expanded*)? How did it go?
2. Share one principle you have tried to implement since this study has begun.
3. Share examples of compartmentalization and middle ground cooking.
4. In general, what qualities do you think healthy families demonstrate? Brainstorm as many as you can.

# ATCH

Every blended family story begins with loss and sadness, at least for someone.

1. An undercurrent of loss and sadness

2. The Israelites' journey through the wilderness

   • Exodus 14:11ff.

   • The typical journey involves many transitions you didn't anticipate.

   • You have to keep walking through the Sea of Opposition.

• Trust God.

# **D**ISCUSS

1. What part of Ron's description of the wilderness wanderings matches your family's experience so far?

2. How does believing that you can make it through the wilderness make a difference in how you live today?

3. The following emotions often make people "look back to Egypt." Which have you experienced and perhaps been tempted by: anger, depression, sadness, longing, hurt, resentment, guilt, fear, rejection? How can you keep these feelings in check? What role could prayer play?

4. What does trusting God at this point in your journey look like for you?

5. Fear in children and adults is a significant saboteur of your journey together. Someone read aloud the section entitled "Don't Look Now; We're Being Pursued" in chapter 1 of *The Smart Stepfamily, Revised and Expanded* and then discuss these questions:

   • Which fears of the biological parent or stepparent can you relate to and why?

   • Consider your losses in life (now and before your marriage). How do your current fears connect with those experiences? How have previous losses sensitized you to pain in current relationships?

   • What fears do you see in your children?

6. Think for a moment about the person in your extended stepfamily that you get along with least well. Share some ways you can communicate commitment to that family member this week.

7. Share a humorous story or occasion from your family. It may have been a situation that you didn't think was funny when it happened, but now, looking back, you can see that it was.

**PPLY**

How will you apply these principles?

**P**RAY

Prayer Requests to Honor This Week:

## **R**EAD

Recommended Reading for This Week:

- *The Smart Stepfamily, Revised and Expanded*, chapter 2
- Consider trying the Travelogue exercise found at the end of chapter 2 of *The Smart Stepfamily, Revised and Expanded* before the next meeting.

# Two-STEP: Your Marriage

## **O**PEN

Before the video:

1. Did anyone try the Travelogue exercise (found at the end of chapter 2 of *The Smart Stepfamily, Revised and Expanded*)? Share what happened and any insights you received.

2. What are some qualities of healthy marriages? Brainstorm a quick list.

3. If you have taken the Couple Checkup, what strengths did it reveal in your relationship? (If you haven't taken it yet, consider doing so at SmartStepfamilies.com.)

4. In general, what are some marital weaknesses you are working on? (Don't share specifics without your partner's permission.)

# ATCH

Two-STEP—the marital relationship

1. There are unique stressors for blended-family couples.

2. Pain from the past can affect the present.

   • Protecting yourself is understandable, but can be debilitating.

   • Trust, vulnerability, and risk.

3. Danger: holding on to your kids and pushing away your marriage will erode trust in your marriage fast.

4. Managing parenting differences

   • Agree how you'll parent

   • Maintain a "both/and" mentality

   • Agree to being "a married couple first"

   • Stepparents: occasionally step back

   • "Leave and cleave" (Genesis 2:24)

5. Caution: Expect pushback from children

   • Have compassion and empathy for them

6. Your marriage is the first and last motivator of bonding in your family.

# DISCUSS

1. The Two-Step is a dance. How well are you dancing together right now?

2. In what ways can you relate to the overprotective father?

3. What "ghost whispers" do you hear?

   • What does the ghost make you do?

   • What helps you manage your ghost?

   • If your ghost were busted and you could love without fear, what is one thing you would begin doing more often?

4. "Leave" in Genesis 2:24 refers to shifting your allegiance to your spouse. "Cleave" refers to commitment. What are ways to live these daily?

5. What response have you seen in your children to your "leaving and cleaving"?

For further study:

- *The Smart Stepfamily Marriage* by Ron L. Deal and David H. Olson and 13-week study guide.
- *The Smart Stepfamily Guide to Financial Planning* by Ron L. Deal, Greg S. Pettys, and David O. Edwards can help you "finance togetherness."

## Ⓐ PPLY

How will you apply these principles?

**PRAY**

Prayer Requests to Honor This Week:

**READ**

Recommended Reading for This Week:

- *The Smart Stepfamily, Revised and Expanded,* chapter 5. An extensive section at the end of this chapter helps you identify and bust your ghosts and offers guidance to spouses as they join in the ghost busting.

Session **6**

# Side STEP Common Pitfalls

## **O**PEN

Before the video:

1. Share a personal victory, i.e., something that is improving in your life or family.
2. What do you think are the most common stumbling blocks for stepfamilies? For couples in stepfamilies?

## **W**ATCH

Side STEP the most common pitfalls stepfamilies face.

1. Underestimating loss
   - Loss is centralizing and enduring


   - The gap between kids and adults can put distance between you quickly.


   What to do:

   - If dating: go slow! If married, don't trade one family for another.


   - Give permission to sadness


   - Model grieving and have grace for the losses of others


   - Stepparents: don't take it personally


   - Biological parents: don't get paralyzed

2. Not working well as a parent and stepparent team

   6 principles of healthy parenting and stepparenting

   • Partner

   • Pursue

   • Pace

   • Patience

   • Persistence

   • Prayer

# A Prescription for Evolving Parent and Stepparent Roles

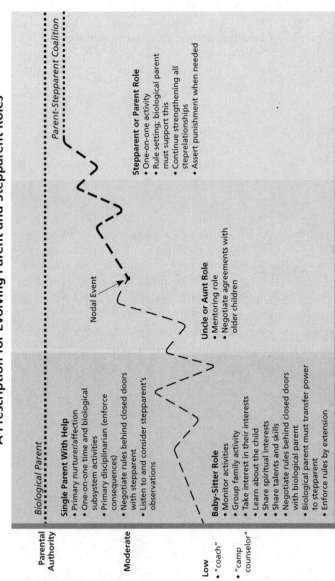

**Parent-Stepparent Coalition**

**Biological Parent**

**Single Parent With Help**
- Primary nurturer/affection
- One-on-one time and biological subsystem activities
- Primary disciplinarian (enforce consequences)
- Negotiate rules behind closed doors with stepparent
- Listen to and consider stepparent's observations

**Stepparent or Parent Role**
- One-on-one activity
- Rule setting; biological parent must support this
- Continue strengthening all steprelationships
- Assert punishment when needed

**Uncle or Aunt Role**
- Mentoring role
- Negotiate agreements with older children

Nodal Event

**Baby-Sitter Role**
- Monitor activities
- Group family activity
- Take interest in their interests
- Learn about the child
- Share spiritual interests
- Share talents and skills
- Negotiate rules behind closed doors with biological parent
- Biological parent must transfer power to stepparent
- Enforce rules by extension

**Parental Authority**

**Moderate**

**Low**
- "coach"
- "camp counselor"

## Time With Stepchildren

Length of time required to increase parental authority will vary according to age of child, previous family experiences, relationship with noncustodial parents, child's temperament/personality, parenting style variations, and child's overall stepfamily satisfaction level.

1. Dr. Susan Gamache, "Parental status: A new construct describing adolescent perceptions of stepfathers" (PhD dissertation, University of British Columbia, 2000).

**Degree of Authority to Discipline[1]**
Interface between "asserted authority" by the stepparent and "accepted authority" by the stepchildren.

# **D**ISCUSS

1. What did you learn about loss and its impact on stepfamilies?

2. How might loss be affecting your child's behavior? What parenting adjustments could you make?

3. What insights did you gain from the "6 P's"?

4. Review and discuss the "Summary Points to Remember" at the end of chapter 7 of *The Smart Stepfamily, Revised and Expanded*. Take time to discuss the application of each to your family.

5. What if you now realize that your system of parenting has been misguided or ineffective? What changes might you make?

   • See "But We're Already Stuck. What Do We Do Now?" at the end of chapter 7 of *The Smart Stepfamily, Revised and Expanded,* for more answers.

## PPLY

How will you apply these principles?

## PRAY

Prayer Requests to Honor This Week:

## READ

Recommended Reading for This Week:

- *The Smart Stepfamily, Revised and Expanded*, chapters 7 & 8.
- Optional: If you have time, also read *The Smart Stepfamily, Revised and Expanded*, chapter 9.

**Session**

**7**

# STEP in Line With the Parenting Team

GROUP NOTE: At the end of this session you will make decisions as to what topics you will discuss during session eight. Be sure to leave ten minutes for this discussion before you dismiss.

## Open

Before the video:

1. What between-home frustrations do you experience?
2. What do you think this phrase means? "There are no ex-parents, only ex-spouses."

## ATCH

STEP in Line with the parenting team.

1. Terms referring to blended families
   - Binuclear

   - Children as citizens in two countries

   - Co-parenting as between-country negotiations

2. If a parent is deceased

3. Diplomacy in co-parenting

   - Kids are naturally in the middle

   - Reduce conflict. Don't be an _____

   - Give kids your permission to love others

   - Don't ask kids to be _____

- Be business-like

- Separate "personal" from "parental"

- Have scheduled "business meetings"

- They need you to take care of _____

4. If spiritual values differ:

   - Do your part

   - Influence

   - Inoculate

   - You may have to endure _____ living

# Ⓓ ISCUSS

1. Who are the adults who make up your "parenting coalition" (i.e., all parents, stepparents, grandparents, and caretakers)?

2. If children are "dual citizens," then they belong in each home. How can you show respect for that reality?

3. Do your children feel your permission to like or love the people in the other home? Under what circumstances does this get tricky for them?

4. Read aloud this poem written by Colleen, age 11, and discuss the questions that follow.

### Which Limb Am I?[1]

I have two sets of parents.
I'm lucky, you say.
Just try being in my shoes
Every other Friday.
"I love you!"
"I love you more!!"
Oh somebody, please somebody,
Get me out of this tug-of-war.
The lawyers and judges,
They all play a part
In creating a torn, shattered, and broken heart.
I know I'm not alone,
There are lots of kids like me
With a horribly complicated family tree.

1. Tom Worthen, ed., *Broken Hearts . . . Healing: Young Poets Speak Out on Divorce,* abridged version (Logan, Utah: Poet Tree Press, 2001), 19. Used with permission.

- What is the impact on children of being caught in an emotional tug-of-war?

- How can you reduce the conflict in your situation?

5. What value differences are there between your child's homes?

   - What tips did you gain from the video regarding spiritual training and your children?

6. Review and discuss the "Guidelines for Co-Parents" in chapter 6 of *The Smart Stepfamily, Revised and Expanded.*

- Which ones might benefit your children?

## PPLY

How will you apply these principles?

## GROUP DECIDE

Next week you have a number of optional topics to discuss. To-gether decide which two or three subjects you will study (and plan to read the corresponding sections in *The Smart Stepfamily, Revised and Expanded* before the next session). You may also decide to meet for more than eight sessions in order to study all of these topics.

1. The impact of unrecognized loss and unexpressed grief on your family (read the section on unrecognized loss and un-expressed grief at the beginning of chapter 9 in *The Smart Stepfamily, Revised and Expanded*).
2. Menacing emotions (read "Driven by Menacing Emotions" in chapter 9 of *The Smart Stepfamily, Revised and Expanded*).
3. Combining holiday and family traditions (read the section on holidays and traditions at the end of chapter 9 in *The Smart Stepfamily, Revised and Expanded*).
4. Unique parenting roles and circumstances, including: adult stepchildren; part-time parenting; the effect of birth order changes on children; stepparenting adolescents; parenting a mutual child; sibling relationships; adopting stepchildren; and legal matters in stepparenting. (Read about each of these

subjects in chapter 8 of *The Smart Stepfamily*, *Revised and Expanded*.)

5. Money matters (read *The Smart Stepfamily*, *Revised and Expanded*, chapter 10).

6. Managing sexual temptations in the stepfamily (read the section on sexuality at the beginning of chapter 11 of *The Smart Stepfamily*, *Revised and Expanded*).

7. How divorce affects children and faith formation (read "Divorce, Remarriage, and Faith Formation" in chapter 11 of *The Smart Stepfamily*, *Revised and Expanded*).

8. You may also want to read and discuss bonus material on a variety of topics available online at SmartStepfamilies.com/view/learn and at the end of this study guide.

## RAY

Prayer Requests to Honor This Week:

## READ

Recommended Reading for This Week:

- *The Smart Stepfamily*, *Revised and Expanded*, chapter 6.
- Read the sections that coincide with your chosen subjects for next week's discussion.

# STEP Over Into
# the Promised Land

**O**PEN

Before the video:

1. Use the discussion questions found at the end of each chapter in *The Smart Stepfamily, Revised and Expanded* to discuss your selected subjects (see chapters 8–11). Record notes below.

Selected Subject 1:

Selected Subject 2:

# ATCH

A quick review:

STEP UP to a God who loves and forgives you

STEP Down your expectations

STEP Through the wilderness with faith

Two-STEP the marital relationship

Side STEP common pitfalls

STEP In Line with all the other adults, so you can . . .

STEP _____ into the "Promised Land"

1. Promised Land rewards:

- Marital _____

- Healthy marriage model for children

- A healthy stepfamily helps restore well-being in children

- Passing the baton of faith

2. How God uses family life to disciple us:

   • God's "choosing love"

3. God can take the fractured, dysfunctional pieces of our life and turn them into a masterpiece (see Ephesians 2:10).

# **D**ISCUSS

1. Which of the Promised Land rewards encourages you most?

2. How has God used your family to deepen your spiritual walk with him?

3. What part of this series has had the greatest impact on you?

4. What key principles will you hold on to?

## Ⓐ PPLY

How will you apply these principles?

## Ⓟ RAY

Prayer Requests to Honor This Week:

# ®EAD

Recommended Reading for This Week:

- *The Smart Stepfamily, Revised and Expanded,* chapter 12.
- Skim the Bonus Material portion of this study guide for questions that speak to your life.
- If you haven't already, review the bonus material on a variety of blended family topics available online at SmartStepfamilies .com/view/learn.

## WHAT'S NEXT?

Next steps for you and your group:

- At this point many groups decide to continue meeting together for further study. Will this be your final meeting or will you continue studying all the optional sections found in *The Smart Stepfamily?* Perhaps you would like to study another resource on stepfamily living (see the list on page 10) or a Bible study. You can also spend time reviewing the Bonus Material in this study guide.
- If you decide to continue meeting, be sure to decide when, where, how often, and who will lead. May God bless your journey together.

# Bonus Material

This section provides bonus study material. It includes:

- Family Meetings: A Tool for Problem Solving, p. 66
- Smart Questions, Smart Answers, p. 69

Additional bonus material can be found online at SmartStepfamilies .com/view/learn.

# Family Meetings:
## A Tool for Problem Solving

The family meeting is an effective strategy for managing issues and pitfalls. This tool can be utilized in a variety of circumstances.

Corporations have strategy meetings on a regular basis. Department heads, supervisors, and managers get together to discuss current production goals, sales reports, and marketing efforts. The purpose behind such meetings is to generate teamwork and improve efficiency and profit as the whole works toward a common goal. Family meetings help stepfamilies do the same. The goals are different (integration, spiritual formation, and generating unconditional love and respect), but the process is similar.

Weekly or biweekly family meetings are the perfect time to process emotions and negotiate preferences, rule changes, discipline consequences, and roles in the home. Vacation plans can be made, rituals for the holidays worked out, and feelings of loss and hurt shared. But perhaps the most unexpected result for many stepfamilies that make use of this tool is a sense of identity. The meeting itself becomes a unique tradition that helps family members listen, spend time with each other, and experience their family being together. You can have meetings on a regular basis or periodically as needed.

## What Is a Family Meeting?

- Time set aside to promote meaningful communication and to provide for family discussion, decision making, problem solving, encouragement, and cooperation.

- Family meetings can be structured and formal or flexible and informal.

- Everyone has a part and something to contribute. Meetings are democratic; that is, everyone has a voice, but not the same decision-making power. Parents have the final say but should empower children to contribute whenever possible.

- Ultimately, family meetings build much needed family traditions, create memories, and establish a working family identity.

## How Do We Get Started?

- The process is easier if meetings begin when children are young (age four or five). Older children may have negative reactions at first, but most come to value the process once they experience the benefits.

- Simply make a decision to start, have a plan of action, and begin.

## General Guidelines for Effective Family Meetings

- Make meetings a priority. They should happen at regular, predictable times (e.g., each Thursday night). Don't allow distractions to diminish your commitment to the process. Establish and stick to time limits.

- Begin each meeting with compliments and words of appreciation when they can be offered genuinely. Encouragement facilitates integration but shouldn't be offered if not sincere.

- Post an "agenda board" (perhaps on the refrigerator) and encourage everyone to contribute to the list. Be sure each item is discussed and equal consideration is given to each concern.
- Rotate leaders so that children have a turn (your teenagers will love being in charge!).
- Honor one another's feelings and opinions. Use your listening skills and speak with respect. Don't permit meetings to become gripe sessions. Seek first to understand, then to be understood.
- Work to find solutions to problem situations. Brainstorm possible solutions and consequences if agreements are not kept. This helps each person take ownership of the problem and its solution. This also clarifies expectations and allows each to experience the stepfamily working together.
- End the meeting with an enjoyable activity. You all may be together or break into mini-family groups, but have ice cream, play mini-golf, or play board games. Make it fun.

# Smart Questions, Smart Answers

The way of a foolish person seems right to him. But a wise person listens to advice.

Proverbs 12:15

For years I have been collecting questions from stepfamilies in an attempt to understand which issues seem to be the most common. This bonus material addresses some pressing questions that have not been specifically answered in *The Smart Stepfamily, Revised and Expanded*. Topics include difficult ex-spouses, the needs of children, co-parenting strategies, stepparenting, military stepfamilies, dealing with family conflict, stepgrandparenting, and more.

I have solicited the expertise of a number of stepfamily researchers, practitioners, and therapists in answering some of these key questions. They have graciously volunteered their wisdom and practical knowledge for your benefit.

## When Does the Integration Period Begin?

Does the seven-year integration period include dating before marriage, or does this period officially begin at the wedding?

Without a doubt, what takes place prior to the wedding, including how much time is allowed for grieving losses and how much time the couple spends dating, impacts the length of time required for integration. However, while dating well does make a difference in the length of time required to integrate stepfamily members, so do the unforeseen emotional and psychological shifts that take place within both children and adults after a wedding.[1] What was once a warm dating relationship is now a legal, psychological tie that brings people from different families into the same house, sharing the same food and toilet paper. It's just not the same as dating.

For example, after the wedding stepparents often feel an increase in spiritual and parental responsibility for children. "Before the wedding they were her kids," said Tom. "I kept my hands off and my opinions to myself. But after we married, I felt like I needed to be a part of what was going on. After all, they were living in my house and interacting with my children." Biological parents may resist an increase in stepparent involvement, perceiving it as a threat to their children. Or the opposite may occur. They may hand off too much responsibility to the new stepparent, since "we're a whole family now." In addition, stepchildren who didn't mind Mom's boyfriend being around may resent their now stepfather getting in the way. And when he was Mom's boyfriend, their biological father didn't say much. After the wedding, however, they may start receiving pressure not to enjoy his presence. These post-wedding psychological shifts represent new territory for the couple. In fact, it may feel as if they've started over in some ways.

The stepparent-stepchild relationship often dictates the speed of the stepfamily integration process (see chapter 7 in *The Smart Stepfamily, Revised and Expanded*). Many factors, including the age of the children and their previous family experiences, affect how quickly a bond develops with a stepparent. Do your homework before the wedding. Date slowly and give yourself and the children

---

1. Scott Browning, "Why Didn't Our Two Years of Dating Make the Remarriage Easier?" *Stepfamilies* (Summer 2000), 6.

plenty of time to grieve losses. Then make the children aware of your decision to marry and give them some time to get used to the idea. Involve them in the wedding when possible.[2] Daily renew your commitment to them and express unconditional love. But keep in mind that real stepfamily life begins with marriage. Many adjustments will have to be made, even in the best of circumstances. Take them one day at a time and keep walking with God.

*For more on dating well and making decisions about marriage, read* Dating and the Single Parent.

## Co-Parenting Meetings

**How is a good co-parenting meeting structured and why is ongoing communication with a co-parent important for the children?**

*Answered by Tammy Daughtry, MMFT*[3]

Ashley (now 33 years old) reflects on her childhood between divorced parents: "I was the spy and the mediator after my parents divorced, but I HATED it when they put me in the middle! I even had to ask for the child support check and why it was late. I always wanted to tell them 'It's not my job to be the parent—you should be the parents!' but I was always too scared."

Marriage ends when two people divorce; however, if those two people have shared children, their parenting roles never end. The divorce ends the marriage, not the role of parenting. For the sake of the children, it is critical for biological parents to communicate and do the hard work of being involved parents. It is not the child's

2. Dr. Roger Coleman has created a medallion that can be given to children during the wedding ceremony. The act reassures children of their place in the new family and symbolically represents the commitment that stepparents make to care for their stepchildren. A wonderful resource for engaged couples: familymedallion .com.

3. Tammy Daughtry, MMFT, founder and CEO of Co-Parenting International, author of *Co-parenting Works! Helping Your Children Thrive After Divorce*, and national advocate for children in single-parent and stepparent homes. Tammy has been a co-parent since 2000 and now has a blended family of six. For more information visit CoparentingInternational.com.

job to be the messenger or the go-between, even if the child is an older teenager. This is a common error made by divorced parents who would rather not talk to each other; however, this is very damaging to children and causes lifelong emotional scars and ongoing confusion when they are forced to be the communication vessel between their divorced parents.

Another situation that hurts children with divorced parents is when parents try to talk at length during the "hand-off" between homes. Many parents will stand at the doorstep of the other's home and ask questions about finances and schedules or argue about holiday plans or unresolved issues between them. Observing conflicted communication causes high anxiety in kids, awkward experiences, and if the conversation gets loud and hostile, it can even jeopardize everyone's safety.

A suggested solution is to have co-parenting "T.E.A.M.M." meetings to work out details between the two homes. The T.E.A.M.M. acronym means "The End Adult Matters Most," which is a critical perspective to uphold when co-parents communicate. The big picture, long-term well-being of the children is always best to keep in mind. The idea is that of being "Co-CEOs" and business partners who have a highly vested interest in the outcome of the common child. CEOs come to meetings prepared with notes, agenda items, ideas to discuss, and positive solutions—they do not allow personal emotions or selfishness to get in the way of objective thinking and planning. Co-parents who want to raise well-adjusted kids can learn from the model of a successful CEO. It takes an intentional partnership to discuss financial decisions, project short-term and long-term goals, and allow others to express their ideas and opinions (even if they are vastly different).

Co-parenting meetings are best done in private, away from the child's visual or audible presence. Co-parenting meetings can be a pre-arranged time to talk by phone once the child is asleep or it can be a meeting in a public coffee shop. Co-parenting meetings can become the safe place to negotiate, disagree, express concern, ask for input, and discuss difficult topics—but never in the presence of the children. This is a strong protective measure divorced parents can put in place to ensure the emotional and physical safety of the children and to enhance the opportunity for parental communication to be ongoing and productive.

Monthly or quarterly meetings are ideal, allowing most communication to be saved for the meetings. This can minimize the times a week the ex-spouses have to talk, text, or email, thus reducing stress in everyone's life. If possible get extra rest the night before so your emotions will be stable. Always think "Kids First and Past Last!" Compartmentalize the discussions to only be about the children and the specific needs of the children; keep the focus on the future, not on the past.

Ultimately what co-parenting meetings achieve (when done in private away from the children) is the ability for kids to transition easily and peacefully between homes and family units. It is a powerful and healing gift to give to children. In addition, when all the biological and stepparents can be present at the child's activities in the same space (e.g., transitions, school functions, special occasions, sports events, extra-curricular activities) the child can relax and *enjoy* all the people they love. A commitment to discuss details only at co-parenting meetings creates a strong and healthy boundary for everyone, including the parents and stepparents. For a free sample of a co-parenting meeting agenda see www.Coparenting International.com.

Suggested topics of discussion can be adjusted according to age and developmental stages of children (for example, age 2 topics include potty training and bedtimes; age 12 might include iPods, cell phones, and social media; age 15 might include driver's permit, driver's training, dating, high school, and paying for college; older children ages 17+ might be issues of the graduation ceremony and celebration, college preparation, moving to the dorm, etc.). There are hundreds of parenting topics that divorced and remarried parents will have the opportunity to discuss. Those discussions can be productive and beneficial to the kids.

## Anger and Unresolved Emotions

**My ex-wife is bad-mouthing my new wife and me. How can we get her to see this is making life more difficult for the kids?**

Anger and unresolved emotions from the previous marital breakup often lead ex-spouses to criticize each other in an effort to gain loyalty from their children or seek revenge for perceived inequalities during the marriage. In addition, my guess is that the biological mother in question is probably feeling threatened by the stepmother's presence. Biological parents need to be reminded that children will always be loyal to them (unless *the parent* cuts off contact). Bad-mouthing a stepmother is unnecessary. Children can respect and obey a stepmother—even care for her deeply—and it won't ever change the strong bond they have with their mom.

To help alleviate this mother's misguided fear, the stepmother and husband should each communicate to his ex-wife their desire to cooperate and not hinder the children's relationship with their mother. The stepmother, in particular, should say in a phone call or email, "I want you to know that your relationship with Beth and Amy is critical to them. Please understand that I will never try to replace you or hinder your relationship with them. In fact, I'm wondering what you would like me to do to help them feel more in touch with you. Do you have any ideas? From this day forward, my commitment to you and the children is to encourage their love and respect for you. If there is anything I can do differently, please let me know." This may or may not impact the mother's criticism, but the hope is that this message will help her to feel less threatened and, therefore, have less need to be negative about the stepmother.

Do what you can to be Christ to anyone in the other home, even if he or she is extremely negative. You may not be able to effect any practical change in an ex-spouse, but don't be guilty of not trying.

*For more on dealing with difficult ex-spouses read* The Smart Stepmom *or* The Smart Stepdad.

## I Don't Like My Stepson

I am feeling like the horrible, evil stepmother. I simply do not like one of my stepsons and I don't want to like him—in part because he reminds me of my verbally abusive ex-husband. I just wish I could find some way to avoid him most of the time.

I appreciate your honesty in addressing this situation. The truth is, sometimes people don't like their stepchildren. You are not the first. Yet, God does call us to "live in peace with everyone," "don't pay back evil with evil," and "overcome evil by doing good" (Romans 12:9–21).

I know this may sound weird, but start working on your relationship with your stepson by forgiving (or forgiving again) your ex-husband. You told me more than you realize when you said, "He reminds me of my verbally abusive ex-husband." You might be emotionally predisposed not to like your stepson because of old bruises that are still sensitive. Heal the bruises with forgiveness, then actively distinguish between what is present (your stepson's behavior) and what is past (your ex-husband's abuse).

The other thing you must do is to pray daily for your stepson. Not just pray about him. You must pray *for* him. He is not your enemy, and your prayers must reflect a growing appreciation for him. Ask God to soften your heart.

By the way, I'm going to make a prediction: when your heart softens toward your stepson, his negative and annoying behavior will decrease (not stop). Most of us are totally unaware of how our judgment toward others incites their negativity toward us.

## Relationships With Adult Stepchildren

How do I develop a relationship with my two stepchildren who were adults when we married?

*Answered by Susan J. Gamache, PhD, R. Psych*[4]

Stepparents coming into a family with grown children can help develop positive relationships with adult children by keeping a few points in mind.

First, there are a wide variety of stepparent-stepchild relationships, ranging from "almost identical to Mom or Dad" to "not at all like Mom or Dad" and everything in between. New stepparents to adult stepchildren need to remember that these young people are far beyond the age when they are available for more parents. However, they can still enjoy a warm, supportive relationship with Mom or Dad's new partner.

Begin by simply noticing what the young person finds meaningful or interesting in life. You do not need to like it yourself to appreciate that it is important to them. You can do a lot for a smooth beginning by accepting them as they are. A word of caution here: The family already has a long history that you cannot change. If you are noticing things that seem strange or uncomfortable for you, speak to your partner about them. Try to understand how it got to be this way. The better you and your partner can communicate about these aspects of family life, the easier it will be for you to compassionately accept the family idiosyncrasies. If things are very strained between your partner and his or her children, you will not be able to fix it. Sometimes just being a "fair witness" to what is going on can be a valuable contribution and can make you a safe person for family members to get close to. However, trying to get the family to change is a good way to alienate everyone.

Second, families go on forever. You have all the time you need to establish warm relationships. If the stepchildren are college age and not terribly interested in family, this is natural. Be patient. Once grandbabies are on the scene, a whole new family life cycle will begin.

---

4. Susan J. Gamache is a registered psychologist and licensed marriage and family therapist in private practice in Vancouver, British Columbia. She is the author of *Building Your Stepfamily: A Blueprint for Success*.

Third, you may find yourself developing stronger ties with young stepgrandchildren than with their parents. In other words, the grandchildren may consider you Granny or Gramps, while their parents don't consider you a parent. This may feel a bit awkward, but it makes perfect sense. Young children are wide open to attachment with adults. Providing your relationship with them is warm and responsive, the young children will include you in their grandparent category. This provides another way to connect with adult stepchildren. Your support of them as young parents will bring you all closer together.

## Military Stepfamilies

**What are some unique stressors for military stepfamilies and what can we do about it?**

*Answered by Todd Gangl, MDiv, former enlisted sergeant and comissioned chaplain, USAFR[5]*

Military stepfamilies face unique stressors. These can include a rigid military lifestyle; frequent moves that lead to separation from friends, family members, and the other biological parent; and the ever-present concern over short- or long-term deployments. Combine these stressors with past studies that have shown that the men and women within our armed forces marry, divorce, and remarry at a younger age and more frequently than their civilian counterparts, and you have a challenging environment in which to blend a family. If you are a military stepfamily, try these tips for overcoming the stress and restoring peace to your blending household.

**The rigid military lifestyle.** Although you or your spouse is a part of a highly disciplined and rigid military unit, your stepfamily

5. Todd Gangl, M.Div, former enlisted USAFR (1986–1990) and chaplain candidate and chaplain, USAFR (1995–2000). Todd and Tammy Gangl are co-founders of Joseph StepFamily Ministries, creators of the StepFamily 411 Seminar, and authors of the upcoming book *The StepFriendly Church*. Learn more at Stepfamily911.com.

is not. In this study you have learned that flexibility, laughter, compassion, and understanding will help your stepfamily to succeed. None of these are taught in basic training. Try this when rigidity invades your home:

- Military structure is for just that, the military. Remember, it is the relationship that you are steadily building with your stepchildren that will allow you the authority to make rules and enforce consequences, not your choice of careers. Be careful not to force military-grade structure onto your stepchildren if you haven't yet earned the right to lead through relationship.

- Starting new traditions is a great way to help your family to blend and to overcome rigidity. Be open to having family meetings and allowing everyone to have input into what new traditions they would like to start.

**Frequent moves.** The military is a transient lifestyle. Frequent moves cause noncustodial parents to face long separations from their children and an increased sense of shame and guilt over not being an active part of their children's lives. Custodial parents who move face isolation from extended family relationships that might lend stability to their family. If you find yourself apart from your children or extended family keep these things in mind.

- If you are a custodial parent, be understanding of your children and stepchildren who are feeling a deep sense of loss over moving from friends and other family members, including a biological parent. Allow them to speak openly and honestly about their feelings without minimizing their loss or reacting to their anger, and make sure to have open paths of communication for the children between your home and their other biological parent. Keep them in contact as much as possible.

- If you or your spouse is the noncustodial parent, help each other to overcome any feelings of anxiety or helplessness over moving away from children by working as a family on a long-distance plan. Include things such as staying in touch through social media, plans for live video messaging, and a calendar that highlights dates the children will have their next face-to-face visit with family members.

**Deployment.** Where there is confusion over family roles there will always be stress; the deployment of a spouse creates high role confusion. Deployment can force stepparents to take on the added role of full-time parent before they or the children may be ready for them to do so. It may also force a stepparent into dealing with an ex-spouse-in-law on highly stressful co-parenting matters. Try the following to lower your family's stress before, during, and after the deployment.

### Before the deployment

- Keep in mind that stepparents have no legal rights and require a notarized power of attorney from the biological parent in order to seek emergency medical treatment, to register step-children for school, or even to sign them up for extracurricular activities. The Judge Advocate General (JAG) on your base can help you with this free of charge. You can also utilize the Medical Permission to Treat a Minor Child form available at SmartStepfamilies.com.
- Be proactive and create a deployment parenting plan with your new spouse and your ex that includes possible events and an agreed upon course of action. Make sure to include picking up and dropping off children or arranging travel if required for visitation, medical emergency notification, payment of any child support, and any other possible issues that could affect your family and your ex while you are away.

### During the deployment

- Keep the deployed spouse updated on what is happening in the house with the understanding that they may not be able to respond to every issue you are facing given the stress they may be under at the time.

- Utilize all of the resources of your base Family Readiness Group and Family Advocacy Programs to help you while your spouse is away. The base chapel is also a great place to get information when you do not know where to turn.

### After the deployment

- Treat the reintegration stage of your deployment the same as you treated your first year as a new stepfamily. Take things slow and easy while gradually making changes back to the way you parented (parent and stepparent roles) before the deployment.
- If needed, seek help early for any family situations that might arise after the deployment. Use Military OneSource, which offers six free, confidential family and individual counseling sessions to active duty soldiers, guard members, and reservists.

## Memories of a Deceased Parent

How do you include memories of a stepson's deceased mother comfortably so he doesn't think everyone has forgotten her, but so that it doesn't inhibit his involvement and acceptance of his new family?

This stepmother's question reveals a common misunderstanding: letting people remember the past or relish its memories will create barriers to future attachments. It does not. Indeed, just the opposite is true. By displaying pictures of the boy's deceased mother and listening to his stories of her life, this stepmother is paving a way for her stepson to accept and respect her. It is not a threat to the new family for them to acknowledge the past. In fact, denying people their memories and sadness goes a long way to sabotaging the new family.

To step forward, this stepfamily will entertain occasional and spontaneous conversations about the mother's death (a typical grieving pattern for children) and be interested in the boy's feelings about her. If he goes through a period of time in which he wants to discuss her frequently, the biological parent should take an active role in the conversations. In effect, the two (including other biological children if present) are grieving together. This is a healthy form of family mourning. A stepparent who encourages and allows such conversation, sometimes in her presence, is giving her new family a wonderful gift over time.

## What to Call a Stepparent

**My son has called his stepfather "Dad" in front of his biological father. His biological father told him not to call his stepfather "Dad," but I guess he has decided he wants to do so. His biological father seems very hurt by the whole incident. I feel that this should be my son's decision to make. What is your opinion and how do I address it with my son and his father?**

Ideally, you are correct. Your son should get to decide what he wants to call his stepdad. However, his father's feelings will surely impact his decision. If he now backs away from calling his stepdad "Dad," then you should not pressure your son to call him that anyway, nor should your husband (stepdad) have his feelings hurt. To do so creates a no-win situation for your son. His loyalties to his biological father will matter a great deal to him. Don't put him in a situation where he risks losing approval from his biological father by pressuring him to go ahead with the "Dad" label.

Some kids find a way around this, for example, by calling stepdad "Dad" when his biological father is not around and then referring to him as "Michael" when he's with his biological father.

Taking off the pressure is important. Say this to your son, "Look, I know this puts you in a tight spot between your dad and your stepfather. You may want to call Michael 'Dad,' but it just might hurt your dad's feelings. I know this is tough. Whatever you want to do is okay with us. The real joy is in your relationship, not the labels."

*For more on labels and the use of names in stepfamilies read The Name Game, SmartStepfamilies.com/view/name-game.*

## Discipline of Nonresidential Children

**What kind of discipline should we have when our daughter visits in the summer? Should we treat her as a visitor and try to keep the peace or establish consequences to be enforced regarding acting-out behaviors and responsibility?**

It is tempting to be permissive with nonresidential children. Biological parents want so badly for their children to feel good about their visit that they frequently exempt them from house rules. This, in effect, forces everyone else in the home to accommodate the visiting child (giving far too much power to a child). This is sure to build resentment between a stepparent and the biological parent or between residential children and the biological parent who is displaying the double standard. The assumption that "taking it easy on them" is the best way to give them a good experience is faulty.

Visiting children should be expected to follow house rules and participate in chores like everyone else. They will need extra reminders of the rules and a little grace space as they make adjustments, but in the end, structure is good for everyone.

*For more on part-time parenting and summer adjustments read 6-Week Summer Sleepover at SmartStepfamilies.com/view/sleepover.*

## A Biological Parent's Rejection

My daughter's father won't call her or pick her up for his weekend visit. When she asks why she can't see her dad, what is the best thing to say?

Watching your child suffer rejection from an uninvolved and uninterested parent is heartbreaking. I've observed that having a parent who promises time together and then repeatedly breaks the promise can be even harder on children. Their hopes are raised only to be dashed on the rocks of disappointment again and again.

Jennifer's father, Roger, lived across the state from her and her stepfamily. He had remarried and had a new son. Roger's new marriage and stepfamily, together with a growing career, took a lot of his time. However, his guilt in not making time to be with his daughter led him to (with good intentions) promise her special weekend visits that never happened.

As Jennifer entered adolescence, she gave constant attention to the horizon, that is, to wondering if her daddy would finally keep his promises. She became increasingly oppositional toward her stepfather and mother and was unmotivated in school. Though previously a good student, her grades were falling fast and so was her mother's tolerance of her behavior. A complicating issue was Roger's subtle invitation for Jennifer to come live with him in a couple years. He conveniently blamed his ex-wife for Jennifer's trouble in school and implied everything would be better when they could finally be together. This kept father and daughter sharing a shallow intimacy brought about by the fantasy of empty promises.

Eventually Jennifer began to ask why her father didn't care to be with her. Her increasing age and cognitive abilities gave her a new ability to see through the empty promises her father had repeated numerous times. When she finally admitted her father's deception, she sank into depression and self-blame. Her mother asked what she should say to help Jennifer.

I reminded her mother that no explanation would take away the pain. Parents cannot take away a child's grief; they can only help them cope with reality. I suggested that it was okay for this mother to share her anger toward Roger, but that she should then turn any conversations toward Jennifer and her feelings. In response to Jennifer's statement, "It's like Dad thinks paying child support is enough," her mother might say, "This is extremely hard for you, huh? It feels like your father doesn't really care. My heart is so sad for you. Tell me more about how you're feeling." Such a response communicates an understanding of her pain and validates her experience. Jennifer's mother should not openly criticize Roger ("He is a selfish man") or make excuses for him ("He's just so busy at work"). Focusing on Jennifer's feelings and helping her to develop a plan for how she will relate to her father is the best approach.

Finally, for those with younger children, a neutral explanation of why a parent is uninvolved works best. "Sometimes moms and dads do things because they don't feel good or because they are confused about what is important. [Now turn the focus back to the child's feelings.] You seem to be feeling hurt over this. Tell me about it."

*Emotional coaching is a vital skill to helping children deal with sadness. Learn more about this at SmartStepfamilies.com/view/emotional-coaching.*

## Severing Bonds With an Ex-Spouse

**My husband's ex-wife seems to rely on him for the most basic needs. My husband talks with his ex-wife often (sometimes daily) to discuss their children. How do I deal with feeling that she is intruding on our new marriage?**

The bonds with ex-spouses are often perpetuated by unhealthy patterns. *The Smart Stepfamily, Revised and Expanded* discusses how anger and pain tie two people together. It is my experience that when ex-spouses are still able to call on each other for personal favors, guilt and obligation are the two emotions at work. In session 7 of this study we discussed the need to sever marital bonds and retain parental ones when spouses divorce. Personal favors, like fixing the lawn mower, comforting an ex who is hurting, or giving financial advice fall within the realm of marital exchanges. When you or your ex-spouse calls on the other for such favors, you are perpetuating an unhealthy bond. One of you has remarried, so there is no longer an obligation to conduct such favors.

New spouses are generally the first to point out what to them is an unhealthy attachment. It makes sense, of course, for them to do so because it feels like a threat to the new marriage. Frequently their spouse will defend their actions or not recognize what is happening. Defensiveness of ongoing personal interaction usually indicates a sense of obligation or guilt that is keeping the patterns alive.

Jim's ex-wife would call him to fix the screen door and he would rush over to do it. His third wife, Ann, couldn't understand why he felt the need and wondered if it represented a flicker of romantic interest in her. But to understand his sense of obligation, look at how the divorce and remarriage occurred. Jim had an affair with Ann that eventually ended his marriage. The affair and remarriage took place during a time of spiritual rebellion. Later, when Jim realized his sin, he confessed, repented, and returned to the Lord. It was at this time that his eyes were opened to the consequences his sin had on both his children and his ex-wife. He couldn't help but feel he had to make it up to them. At the same time, his ex-wife still longed for Jim to come home. Her emotional attachments to Jim were very strong, and she enjoyed any opportunity to talk with him. Disguising her interest with issues related to the children, she would call Jim and ask for personal favors like fixing the door. Jim would respond, thinking, *I've left her without someone to help her. I need to do this for her.* What Jim didn't realize was that responding to his ex-wife's requests fed her interest in him, resulting in more and more requests.

While the spiritual and practical consequences of Jim's affair and divorce are tremendous (particularly for his children), the truth of the matter is this: He is now married to Ann and should honor that commitment completely. Yes, his relationship with his children is important, and he should strive to be the best father and co-parent possible. His obligation to cooperate with his ex-wife regarding the children is still in place. However, a line should be drawn between parental and marital issues.

The next time a request is made, Jim should take time to evaluate (he doesn't have to give his ex an immediate answer on the phone) whether it is a parental or personal (marital) issue. If it is personal, he needs to respond kindly and respectfully with a *no*. For example, "I know in the past I would help you with house maintenance, but I don't think fixing the screen door is my obligation. I'm going to have to say no this time. How did Mark do on his math test?"

Finally, conversations about the children can be excessive and, therefore, personal as well. The amount of time that you and your ex-spouse speak about the children can create a false personal intimacy. Let your co-parental conversations be respectful and businesslike, and only as long as necessary. Then invest your extra time in your children and new marriage.

## Reducing Friction and Tension

What is my role as the biological parent in reducing friction and tension in our home?

*Answered by Craig A. Everett, PhD*[6]

Stepfamilies do not often work well as democracies, even when the children are adolescents. Some form of hierarchy for the parents is necessary, particularly in the early stages of forming a stepfamily (perhaps over the initial two years together). In most stepfamilies it is hard for the stepparent to assume much power or authority over the other parent's children. Even if this were possible, it would not be recommended because the needs of the children dictate that they

6. Craig A. Everett is a marital and family therapist in private practice and co-director of the Arizona Institute for Family Therapy, Tucson, Arizona. He is co-author of *Healthy Divorce: Fourteen Stages of Separation, Divorce, and Remarriage* (Jossey-Bass, 1994/1998).

have time to become familiar with and accept the new stepparent into their lives. The process of accomplishing this will vary greatly among families and often depends on the following six issues:

1. The ages and relative maturity of the children
2. The children's preparation for and adjustment to their parents' divorce
3. The manner in which the stepparent was introduced to the children following the divorce (or before in some cases)
4. The stepparent's relative comfort, patience, and personal resources in dealing with these stepchildren
5. The ability of the biological parent to balance her/his new role as a spouse with the continuing role as a parent
6. The relative support (as compared to sabotaging) for the biological parent and for the stepfamily that is displayed and communicated to the children by their other biological parent

Even when remarried parents have completed family therapy and/or educational programs to enhance their understanding of stepfamily dynamics and to improve their communication and decision making, the biological parent must remain in control of the parenting team and have the recognized power to structure and discipline when necessary. The biological parent's power can be defined and negotiated in private consultation with the stepparent. But when the stepfamily is interacting, the biological parent's power must be clearly understood and respected by the children and the stepparent.

In stepfamilies with high levels of friction and tension, particularly after the early transitions, this hierarchy is often unclear and weak. The children may perceive that their parent is in continual conflict over parenting with the stepparent. They may perceive that their parent has given authority to the stepparent, whom they neither know nor trust. They may also react toward what they perceive to be an intrusion by the stepparent into their lives and home. The biological parent may feel unsupported by his or her partner in parenting issues, and the stepparent may feel uninvolved and useless in the family.

All of these dynamics in a stepfamily can lead to internal friction and tension. The biological parent, in consultation with the new partner, needs to assert a sense of leadership and maintain a clear parenting hierarchy so that the children can feel safe and their lives can feel predictable.

Dr. Everett has offered good advice. And because this issue is a common one for biological parents, I'd like to tackle it from another angle. *Triangulation* is a term used by family therapists to describe a relational process between three people. The triangle typically involves two people whose relationship is unstable and a third person whose presence adds stability by diffusing the two-person discomfort. (Sounds technical, doesn't it?) Here's how triangulation frequently works in a stepfamily.

A stepparent and a stepchild begin to get on each other's nerves, perhaps by criticizing each other or being uncooperative. In order to bring stability to the tension, the biological parent intervenes and coaches the two parties on how to better get along. After all, who better to intervene than the one person who has a vested interest in everyone liking one another, right? Wrong. The triangulation process brings temporary stability to the two-person conflict, but sometimes it creates long-term difficulties.

While triangles can be helpful during a time of transition, a habitual pattern of triangulation can actually prevent problem solving. Biological parents should seek the delicate balance of supporting and listening to the two parties without becoming their rescuer. When a biological parent is forced into bridging every gap between a stepparent and stepchild, the two cannot ever bridge the gap themselves—they are dependent upon the biological parent for help. The irony of this pattern is that the conflict is actually extended long-term due to the biological parent's involvement.

Reducing tension occurs when listening to a child's frustration is balanced with validating his concerns (without necessarily agreeing with the child's position, because agreement forms a dangerous parent-child alliance against the stepparent). It means saying, "It's time for you and Bob to work this out. Let me know how it goes." Likewise, Bob may express his frustrations about his stepchild, but still needs to find a way to build a bridge to the child and resolve the conflict.

This same principle applies to stepsibling (and sibling) conflict. An adult who always intervenes in child conflict robs the children of the opportunity to negotiate, learn to make trades, or find other solutions to their problems. Someone complains, "Mom, Jared took my video game without asking." Instead of offering a solution, de-triangulate yourself and encourage the two to resolve the problem. Say, "I can see you're upset. What did Jared say when you spoke to him about that?" When the child says, "Nothing. I haven't said anything to him," you say, "Then maybe you should. I'm sure you can work this out." Then monitor the conversation from a distance. Eventually they will establish their own bridge and their own relationship.

Wanting your decision to remarry to bring joy to your children and spouse—and not pain—means wanting everyone to get along. *Not every person in your stepfamily will be happy all the time. Learn to live with other people's anxiety and unhappiness.* Even though it makes you uncomfortable, their anxiety with one another actually helps motivate them to change. If you try to help them feel better all the time, you rob them of a much-needed motivator for change.

## Fair Treatment of Biological and Stepgrandchildren

How do you get grandparents to be fair toward their stepgrandchildren?

Grandparents frequently find themselves in awkward situations. Loyalty conflicts lead them to make inadvertent and purposeful decisions that reflect their close ties. For example, out of loyalty to their son, grandparents may not spend much time with grandchildren who have primary residence with their former daughter-in-law. Or the awkwardness of supporting their biological grandchildren through a difficult time of transition may lead them to be less than fair in Christmas gift-giving. To give equally expensive gifts to grandchildren and stepgrandchildren may feel like a betrayal toward their grandchildren, who are already feeling loss in the stepfamily.

No matter the motivation for previous grandparent behavior, biological parents have the responsibility to communicate their expectation that grandparents treat each child the same. This may put grandparents in an even more awkward situation (in their minds), but the standard of fairness or equity remains. Note that it is the biological parent's obligation to articulate this expectation; in most situations the stepparent doesn't carry enough clout to make the request.

To set the boundaries, say something like, "I know our situation may not be exactly as you would have it, and you can really help out the kids by doing a few things. Please treat all the children equally in things such as gift-giving and attending performances and celebrations. You can spend time with Josh and Julie [biological grandchildren] without Maddie and Camron [stepgrandchildren]. Over time, let's let Maddie and Camron show us how much time they would like with you. If they are open to it, you can really support our family by spending some time with them. I know sometimes you get in a tight spot between me and the other household, so if you ever have questions, please don't hesitate to call."

In some situations, the boundaries have been clearly articulated, but the grandparents are not interested in honoring them. You may have to set even firmer ones. "We have spoken a number of times about fair gift-giving at birthdays, but you continue to spend lots of money on Josh and Julie and barely any on Maddie and Camron. Until you can acknowledge all the children in our family fairly, we will not allow you to give gifts to any of the kids.

This is important to our family and to the kids. We hope you can comply." Sometimes standing up for your family means drawing lines in the sand and sticking to them.

## To Spend or Not to Spend: Keeping Up with the Other Parent

My stepson's mother tends to buy for him excessively. He has all of the newest and best electronics, and every time he shows an interest in something she runs out and buys him everything he will need to pursue that interest. I have a son who is nine months younger. My stepson's mom pays for things that we cannot afford to do for my son. I can tell this is going to be a source of ongoing tension in our home. What do we do?

Your situation is a frustrating one. However, at the heart of this I would encourage you to think of it as similar to when your son's close friends get a new car, etc., and he doesn't. There will be lots of, "Mom, why can't I have that?" complaining in the future in relation to his friends as well. So, no, you don't give in and let the bio mom's spending habits dictate your own. Stand firm in your convictions (although you will surely have a lot of complaints to deal with from your son).

Tell him the truth without becoming overly critical of your stepson's mother. Say to your son, "I realize it is difficult for you to stand by and watch your stepbrother get everything he wants. His mother has a different value system than we do about spending money on things. Let me explain why we believe the Lord wants us to make the choices we've made. . . . [Explain your thinking and priorities with a faith perspective.] Your stepbrother's mom has decided to make different choices. That's up to her. But we are choosing to do this. I appreciate your bringing this to my attention. I know it's tough. What are your thoughts? [Continue to dialogue.]"

## Pictures From the Past

I am divorced with two children, ages 11 and 9. In your seminar you mention that it is important to allow children to have pictures of their past in their home or rooms. Should the pictures be with the children and their mom or with me included?

Ideally you shouldn't dictate what kind of pictures the kids choose to put up in their own personal space. I know it's hard for your new wife to see you in a picture with your ex-wife, but to be honest, she looks at the fruit of that union every day (the kids!). Your wife needs to accept this; being a stepparent means accepting that someone came before her.

By the way, keep all things in balance. If your kids want to hang a six-foot portrait of their mother over the fireplace mantel, you can say no.

## Differences Between Children

How do you blend children with personalities that are so different? It seems as if I am favoring my child and overly punishing my stepchild.

*Answered by Francesca Adler-Baeder, PhD[7]*

This question is often asked by a parent in a first family about siblings and by a stepparent about stepsiblings. Children are unique individuals from the day they are born, interacting differently with their environments (and the people in those environments). Although we tend to think of parenting as something we do to children (a unidirectional model of influence), in fact, parenting is a bi-directional model of influence, meaning there is action and reaction going both ways. It makes sense, then, that each parent-child

7. Francesca Adler-Baeder, PhD, CFLE, Professor and Extension Specialist, Department of Human Development and Family Studies; Director, Center for Children, Youth, and Families and the National Stepfamily Resource Center, Auburn University, Auburn, Alabama.

relationship has its own characteristics. Viewing parenting in this way explains why it is very difficult to interact with all children in one family exactly the same way. Differences are to be expected. The difficulty is that children become very astute at comparing and picking up on differences. They label these differences as preferences, better or worse treatment, or "you love her more," rather than as simply different relationships. They are also generally not capable of acknowledging or even understanding the part they play in the relationship and in your behaviors.

With sibling relationships, comparisons should be addressed by the parent with reassurances that one child is not loved more than the other, but that each one is loved differently. In stepfamilies, responses are more complicated. In most cases a parent does have stronger emotional attachment and love for his or her biological child than the stepchild. It is okay to admit this to yourself. Step relationships take time to develop, and love relationships don't always develop between a stepparent and a stepchild; don't allow yourself to be pushed into comparing a child with a stepchild. For example, a response to a stepchild's accusation (or question) might be, "I have a different relationship with every member of this family. I don't compare them. Every member of this family is cared for, respected, and valued. We have family rules and values that apply to every person in this family."

So yes, you may be more attached to your biological child than your stepchild, and yes, different children's behaviors may elicit different responses from you. That said, there is still much that an adult can do to promote fairness and to give children (both biological and stepchildren) feelings of being cared for and valued.

Check that your labels for the children don't drive your responses and exaggerate qualities. In many families, there appears to be a good kid, who works to please parents, and a bad kid, who is more spirited and tends to push the limits. Over time, labels (created either consciously or subconsciously by parents) set up a cycle of expected behaviors. We find validation for those expectations and express the label to the child in some form, which, in turn, sets up the child to live up to the label. "You're so lazy," "You forget everything—you have no sense of responsibility," and "You *stay* in trouble" become self-fulfilling prophecies. Also, when these attributions develop, it is highly likely that parents don't see or don't focus on behaviors to the contrary. One technique for counteracting this phenomenon when a negative cycle is established is to consciously verbalize the response "That's not like you" and then label the child what you want her to be: "You're a thoughtful person; it's not like you to walk into your sister's room and take a sweater without asking." It is much more likely that the child will begin to live up to the positive labels.

Notice positive behavior. Sometimes children establish patterns of negative behavior because this behavior gets attention—and negative attention is better than no attention. "Catch them being good" is a guideline for parenting in the early years and should be a parenting tool throughout development. Research tells us that increasing the number of positive interactions decreases the number of negative interactions in a relationship (this is true in marriages as well). Make a point of spending more one-on-one time with your stepchild in positive activities. You may begin to see more balance in the child's behaviors and your responses to them.

Establish family rules and be consistent in enforcing them. It is much better to have a plan for behavior management than to think of consequences on the spot when misbehavior occurs. This is an especially useful approach for new stepfamilies, since stepparents should ease into a disciplinarian role with stepchildren. Enforcing "rules of the house" the way that a baby-sitter or other caregiver would is recommended for stepparents. Rules and consequences can be established with children's input. Following through, then, can be matter-of-fact. Consistency is the key to fairness among children in the household: similar responses to similar behaviors. If one has more consequences than the other, it will be understood that this is a result of their choices, not differences in your feelings for them.

## Bullying Within the Stepfamily

**What do you do when your child is bullying his stepbrother? It is hard not to defend my son or blame my stepson.**

*Answered by Sandra Volgy Everett, PhD*[8]

Aggressive behavior—bullying—toward other family members cannot be tolerated, regardless of whether the children are biological or stepchildren. Often in stepfamilies these conflicts among the children are symptomatic of difficulties the family as a whole is having in becoming attached and bonded. Such conflicts may also indicate that the adults are having difficulty creating a united co-parenting partnership. The feelings of loyalty that parents and children have toward each other often lead to differences in how discipline is understood and carried out. When your role as step-parent differs from your role with your own children, resentment and bitterness between family members can result. Of course, this can affect other areas of family functioning as well.

It is important to manage your discipline issues consistently with all the children in your family; have equal expectations based on ages and ability levels. If a child is bullying another child, take a firm stance against such aggression and create appropriate, consistent consequences for the aggressing child, whether the child is a biological child or a stepchild. It is also important to teach your children to work out their differences and feelings within a family discussion (or family meeting) rather than in an aggressive manner.

Stepfamilies often find it difficult to create appropriate discipline methods because of the history each family brings to the new stepfamily. Each is accustomed to the way discipline was handled in their prior family, and neither wishes to give up the familiarity of those methods for new ones that may not feel as comfortable or predictable. Initially, children will often resent new discipline

8. Sandra Volgy Everett is a clinical and child psychologist and family therapist in private practice and co-director of the Arizona Institute for Family Therapy in Tucson, Arizona. She is co-author of *Healthy Divorce: Fourteen Stages of Separation, Divorce, and Remarriage* (Jossey-Bass, 1994/1998).

methods, especially if those methods are more structured, consistent, or rigid than the methods they knew previously. It will help them to accept the new methods if their biological parent promotes and encourages acceptance, and if the two of you present a united front regarding the new manner in which issues will be handled.

One of the things that drew Tim to Maria was her ability to plan and structure her life. Tim had always struggled to be organized in his life and work—and in his parenting. Maria's ability to structure the family schedule and create a higher expectation for behavior had definite advantages, yet it also created many conflicts. Tim's children were not used to her high standards, nor did they take kindly to her expectation that they, too, become organized with their possessions and schoolwork. In the end, Maria kept trying to hold the children to a level of accountability that Tim would not support. Conflict between their children was common, and both parents felt defeated by the other.

Help your children accept new discipline and parenting methods by defining them in a family meeting. This way, children can have input and express their opinions. Open discussion allows for the expression of their frustration and for learning communication methods that may keep them from resorting to aggressive means of resolving disputes.

## Respect for a Stepparent

My stepson doesn't follow rules or treat me with respect. My spouse feels this is allowing him the freedom to express his emotions. What should I do? How do I explain the double standard to my children?

The first issue here is the stepparent's authority. If this situation is happening within the first few years, a number of things must be in place to empower this stepparent (see chapter 7 in *The Smart Stepfamily, Revised and Expanded*). However, let's assume the couple is working together to establish household rules and that the biological parent has communicated them clearly. Let's also assume the biological parent has communicated an expectation that the stepparent is the adult in charge when the biological parent is not present and that they should be treated with respect. What else, then, is happening?

Communicating an expectation of respect for the stepparent but then allowing misbehavior and excusing it as "freedom of expression" is a double standard that will sabotage the stepfamily's integration. Either a difference in parenting style or strong emotion is driving this biological parent. He may not really agree to the household rules or may be concerned about his son's anger over his marriage. However, preserving his relationship with his son by sabotaging his wife's position (by not requiring respect and obedience) brings more long-term harm than good. It not only undercuts the stepmother's power, it forces a double standard on his stepchildren. Furthermore, it slowly erodes the marriage as she comes to learn he can't be trusted to support her in the family. This is not good.

Approach your husband and inquire about his fears for his son. The temptation is to approach your husband and explain why he is treating you poorly and sabotaging your position in the family. However, that is sure to instigate defensiveness on his part (you've probably already tried that, and it didn't work; why would it work now?). Try a different approach. Focus on what he is feeling and what is driving his behavior. Help him wrestle with his fears or concerns. Then, when he feels you are on his side, explain how his behavior is harming his son (not you) long-term by destabilizing your stepfamily. Gain his cooperation and work together to find a solution. If necessary, seek outside help. Someone else may have a voice with your husband that you simply don't have.

## When Kids Lie to the Other Household

We have a stressful co-parent relationship. Now we have discovered that my husband's kids are going back and telling their mom lies about us. We live in a small town and hear this through the grapevine.

We have no idea what to do. Do we confront the kids, or ignore it? It is so hard to watch my loving husband being hurt over and over.

Your husband can be direct in talking to his kids about what they are saying; you should carefully decide with your husband whether you should be involved in the conversation or not based on the strength of your relationship with the stepchildren. What you have from the grapevine is hearsay; don't trust it too much. When you talk to the children leave open the possibility that you don't understand the full picture. For example: "It's my understanding that you have told your mom [fill in the details]. Please tell me about this." Then wait and let them talk. Don't accuse until you've had time to hear them out.

Then, and only if it's still appropriate, your husband can say, "I must say I'm confused about this. First of all, it hurts me very much that you would share things that aren't true with your mother. I understand how you get caught in the middle between our households. I know you are in a stuck place sometimes. But misrepresenting things to your mom only complicates how well our households cooperate together. This hurts me and I wish you'd stop. Help me understand why this happens." Then wait and listen.

This is honest, direct, and sensitive to them being in the middle, yet still sends a strong message of "Please don't do this anymore."

## A Hostile Noncustodial Parent

How do you deal with a hostile noncustodial biological mother (my ex-wife) who paints a wicked picture of us ("they are bad and selfish")? My wife (stepmother) doesn't stand a chance. Not only are conversations with my ex very one-sided (her way or no way), but the children are obviously influenced by her.

*Answered by Jean McBride, MS, LMFT*[9]

9. Jean McBride is president and CEO of the Colorado Center for Life Changes. She is in private practice in Fort Collins, Colorado, where she specializes in issues

Remarried couples face many challenges as they bring their new stepfamily together and begin to take steps to actually feel like a family. Perhaps one of the most complicated and emotionally charged of these challenges is dealing with the children's other parent. Until recently there have been almost no models of how parents and stepparents can work together for the good of the children. Instead, people have operated from more of a fear-based, adversarial position, where biological parents and stepparents competed for the coveted title of "real parent" in the eyes of the children. To effectively address this question, there are a number of points to consider.

Research tells us that stepmothers have a more difficult time establishing relationships with their stepchildren than do stepfathers. There are several reasons for this. The role of mother brings with it an automatic respect and reverence. In addition, a cultural mythology says "Mothers always know how to care for their children," and "A mother's touch will make everything better." This is a tough act for a new stepmother to follow. Biological mothers often fear that stepmothers are replacing them, which creates enormous anxiety and jealousy. In turn, stepmothers feel unimportant, devalued, and often invisible. Children feel the tug-of-war between their mother and stepmother and do their best to get out of the middle. To a child's way of thinking, liking a stepmother often translates into being disloyal to a biological mother.

Divorce is a complicated and multifaceted event in the life of a family. Each member of the family may experience intense feelings of loss, sadness, grief, anger, loneliness, despair, fear, and abandonment, to name just a few. There also may be feelings of relief, hope, and freedom. Intense feelings are often demonstrated through actions. In the question above, there is a good chance that the biological mom is communicating her feelings through her hostility and attempts to get the children on her side.

---

related to divorce, remarriage, and stepfamily life. Jean is the author of *Encouraging Words for New Stepmothers, Hopeful Steps: A Gentle Guide for the Stepfamily Journey* (audio), and *Quick and Easy Brochures About Divorce*.

How does a new stepfamily stand a chance of succeeding in the face of this kind of pressure? Here are a few suggestions:

Develop an attitude of compassion for everyone in the family. There are no easy roles here. Children, biological parents, and stepparents all struggle to do the best they can under the circumstances.

Focus on the things over which you have control. For example, a stepmother can choose to react to what the children's mother says and does, or she can spend her energy more productively getting to know her stepchildren and letting them get to know her. Allow this "getting to know you" period to be slow and gentle with few expectations. Some events will go well and others will not. Accept both as part of the normal development of a stepfamily.

Remember the adage "Slow and steady wins the race"? Children respond best to structure and predictability. For a new stepfamily, sometimes the best course of action is to simply keep at it.

Plan for time together as a couple. Build into your weekly schedule time to connect with each other, even if it is only a shared cup of tea or a quick walk around the block. When the couple is strong, the partners can handle just about anything.

Plan for time alone. Take good care of yourself. Carve out a bit of alone time where you can recharge your emotional and physical batteries. Be ruthless about your self-care.

Set good boundaries. Make every effort to communicate well and cooperate with the children's other parent. And at the same time, be clear about your own boundaries. Know where you are able to compromise and where you aren't. Keep the tone of the interactions businesslike and focused on solving problems.

Keep the children out of disagreements. Handle the business of co-parenting without involving the children. Avoid calling the other parent names or setting her up to look bad in the eyes of the children. Don't get snagged by the temptation to act as badly as the other parent does.

Expand your sense of humor. Focus on the joy in your life instead of the misery. Set a goal to laugh with your family every day.

# Group Leader Notes

W elcome, group leaders!

## Leading With Purpose

I have two goals for this series: providing solid stepfamily education and giving couples a supportive community of faith in which to apply the educational principles learned. The video and discussion guide will provide education; your role is to facilitate a supportive community of faith.

Central to leading effective groups (or teaching Bible classes) is facilitating a safe environment where people can interact with one another, process the content they are learning, and find support as they strive to apply the principles to their lives. In order to facilitate that safe environment, spend a little time in your first few sessions discussing the below group guidelines (also provided to group members in the Welcome section of this study guide). Asking everyone to agree or covenant with one another to abide by the guidelines creates a shared expectation of how group members will interact with one another. This deepens trust and, therefore, the level of support experienced.

After discussing and agreeing to the guidelines, I encourage you to proactively remind group members of them during sessions

## Group Guidelines

1. **Confidentiality**—We agree that what is said here stays here. We honor one another's privacy and will not share stories or details heard in the group meeting with people who are not in attendance.
2. **Honor**—Couples agree not to share intimate details without first asking our partner whether it is okay to share with the group. If you're not sure it's okay to share, then it probably isn't. Wait and ask your spouse outside of the group.
3. **Advice**—We agree not to offer unsolicited advice to one another. If after telling about a frustration someone receives advice, they might feel judged and pressured to abide by the advice. This creates a sharing barrier for them and others in the future. Agree to give advice only if someone first asks for the group's input.
4. **Respect**—We agree to show common courtesy to one another. Examples include allowing everyone to talk (not dominating the group discussion time), not interrupting, not engaging in side conversations during the group discussion, and showing up on time. Even making a commitment to regular attendance shows respect to others who are counting on us to be there. Call if you cannot attend a session.
5. **Acceptance and Encouragement**—We agree to build one another up in the Lord. We will share our faith, love, and support and strive to "walk alongside" one another in mutual encouragement. If we disagree, we will continue to love in spite of our differences.

two and three. Sharing a case study is a good way to do this. For example, to emphasize confidentiality you might share the following at the end of the second session: "Thanks, everyone, for your participation. I'm really enjoying our time together. In fact, I've found myself eager to share with others the good things that are going on here, but I'm reminding myself to be careful with the details. To honor our commitment to confidentiality I'm not sharing what anyone is saying here, just a general comment about what we are studying and that I am learning a lot from this group. Thanks again and we'll see you next week."

## Effective Group Leadership

Effective group leadership is rooted in the art of asking good questions. Your role is not that of an instructor who answers everyone's questions. Rather, view your role as one of a facilitator who asks questions and allows the group to process answers based on the instruction of the video and book.

I suggest you schedule 90 minutes for your group meeting to allow ample time for group members to process and apply what they are learning. Groups with less time will likely need to omit some questions. Also, if your group has plenty of enthusiastic dialogue you may decide to plan for two meetings for every session. Feel free to adapt your schedule and the number of sessions to meet the needs of your group.

Finally, empower your group. Let your group make decisions that affect the group. For example, initially most people only want to commit to attending for eight sessions. But at the end of that time, because bonds have developed between group members, participants may want to continue meeting. Try to empower them to do so. You can study the remaining portions of *The Smart Stepfamily, Revised and Expanded Edition,* the Bonus Material in the second half of this guide, or return to specific sections already covered in the DVD. If the group reaches this type of consensus, help them to continue to meet.

## A Study Guide for Everyone

Each person in your group should have a copy of this study guide (two per couple). Given differences in life experience, roles, and gender, it is important that individuals are able to take the notes that are most important to them. The DVD presentation is under copyright and cannot be copied, so you'll need to purchase another DVD if you have two groups at once or if you plan to loan DVDs out to couples who missed a session.

## Encourage Extra Reading in *The Smart Stepfamily* Book

Nearly two decades of stepfamily ministry has taught me that couples need to hear significant key principles of successful stepfamily living repeatedly before they begin to take root. Many key principles differ greatly from what they already believe about family life; to receive maximum impact, participants need to hear these new principles again and again.

Strive to give couples "three hearings." Watching the video presentation is one hearing, discussing the principles within your group is a second, and reading about the principle after the meeting is a third. Therefore, make sure that couples get a copy of *The Smart Stepfamily: Seven Steps to a Healthy Family, Revised and Expanded Edition* (one copy per couple is fine). This discussion guide provides recommended readings after each lesson and on occasion references the book during group discussions. Encourage couples to have the revised and expanded edition of the book; this guide best corresponds to that edition and provides the latest material and research for your discussion. Plus, you'll want everyone reading the same material so they can discuss it together. Books are available online and through local bookstores.

A Spanish translation of the book entitled *Tus Hijos, los Míos, y Nosotros* is also available.

## Encourage Empathy Skills

In the section Getting the Most From This Series I encouraged group participants to practice empathy during group discussions.

At times group participants will have similar feelings, but may also have very different feelings or experiences. Model empathy within your group and encourage group members to try to put themselves in the shoes of others in order to validate feelings and identify with others. This is a vital skill for healthy stepfamily interaction, so fostering the skill during group time increases the likelihood that group participants will repeat the skill at home (two good examples are biological parents having empathy for the struggles of stepparents and stepparents having empathy for the fears of children).

## Encourage the Online Couple Checkup

Taking the online Couple Checkup from SmartStepfamilies.com brings added value to couples. You will find that couples appreciate this "x-ray" of their relationship and the direction it provides. Three reactions are common:

1. Couples are encouraged. Many couples feel affirmed after taking the profile. It identifies their strengths, confirms their good feelings, and adds confidence.
2. Couples are educated. Many couples will be surprised by something in their report. They may have thought an aspect of their relationship was healthy only to discover that it really isn't. This provides direction for how they can intentionally improve their relationship. If you take time in your group to process what couples learned about themselves, couples will learn from one another.
3. Couples receive early detection. Like a breast exam that identifies a small lump that needs medical attention, some couples will realize after receiving their results that they need personal help. They may talk to you about finding a counselor, pastor, or mentor who can help them with some problems in their relationship.

Finally, I recommend that you take the Couple Checkup first so you can speak more thoroughly about the process and feedback report, and therefore, encourage others to take it. Simply go to SmartStepfamilies.com and click the Couple Checkup link.

## Pre-Stepfamily Counseling

Ministry leaders and mentors conducting individual pre-stepfamily counseling with couples can use this video series as a structured educational tool. Please note that *The Smart Stepfamily* also has discussion questions at the end of each chapter for couples planning to marry and form a stepfamily. For more on effective pre-stepfamily counseling, visit SmartStepfamilies.com/view/counselor.

## Leader Preparation Steps

To adequately prepare yourself to lead group sessions, follow these suggested steps.

1. Review the session outline. Sessions typically begin with an opening discussion question (marked with an "Open" icon) to set the stage for the video presentation. Plan on spending 7–10 minutes welcoming everyone, sharing announcements, praying for your time together, and working through these questions.
2. Preview the video ("Watch") and review the discussion questions ("Discuss"). Feel free to add questions based on your own insights or to target the needs of your group members. Video presentations vary in length, so plan for your discussion time to vary. Devote the bulk of your session time to the Discuss section. This is where principles take on life. To stimulate sharing, be prepared to share your responses first.
3. The application questions ("Apply") are critical to helping people decide how they will utilize the information learned.

Encourage members to verbalize their action plan when possible.

4. Pray over your time together ("Pray"). This encourages group members to be mindful of one another through the week and invites the Holy Spirit to empower change and growth.

5. Read the corresponding chapter in *The Smart Stepfamily, Revised and Expanded Edition* ("Read"). Group members are assigned this reading after each session, but it will be helpful if you have read chapters *before* the meetings. Reading the book will give you additional insights to share during group discussions and will boost your understanding of the principles shared in the video presentation.

6. Consider attending the Summit on Stepfamily Ministry. Learn more at FamilyLife.com/blended.

## Additional Thoughts:

- Have someone prepare refreshments for group members to enjoy during the video. Simple finger foods or a dessert generally works best.

- Before the first session have copies of the Study Guide available for each participant. Remind participants to bring this Study Guide and their copy of *The Smart Stepfamily* each week.

- Within the first two meetings try to connect with group members by phone, email, or text to thank them for attending and to make sure they feel comfortable in the group.

- Create a social media group page (e.g., Facebook) so participants can post comments, share prayer requests, and connect throughout the study—and stay connected after.

- Occasionally remind group members to transfer key action steps for their family to the My Action Plan page at the end of this study guide. This helps them keep track of key applications and learning principles.

- Special note for session 7: Before closing this session your group will need to decide what optional topics you will discuss during session 8. Session 7 includes a list of topics and directions for the "Group Decide." Whereas participants normally read sections in *The Smart Stepfamily* after each session, be sure to point out to participants that this time they will read sections *before* your discussion in session 8. Use the questions provided at the end of each chapter in *The Smart Stepfamily, Revised and Expanded Edition* to discuss each section.

- Encourage participants to tap into the articles, conference events, and online videos available at FamilyLife.com and SmartStepfamilies.com. Participants can receive daily encouragement if they "Like" FamilyLife Blended and Smart Stepfamilies on Facebook or other social media sites.

- Finally, many groups discover that as they approach the last session they don't want to stop meeting together. Your Group Decide in session 7 is a good time to address this. If group members want to meet longer than eight sessions, we suggest you begin making plans to allow them to do so.

## Next Steps: Recommended Follow-up Study

After completing this study, consider leading your group through *The Smart Stepfamily Marriage* and small-group study guide. While *The Smart Stepfamily DVD* examines the broad stepfamily journey, *The Smart Stepfamily Marriage* and study guide focuses in on the couple's relationship and attempts to strengthen them as they lead their family. Purchase books and copies of the study guide at FamilyLife.com.

In addition, consider hosting a stepfamily training event with Ron Deal or via the web. Livestream Blended and Blessed events can be hosted by your church and previous events can be accessed online. Learn more at BlendedandBlessed.com.

## My Action Plan

Ron L. Deal is a marriage and family author, speaker, and therapist. He is founder of Smart Stepfamilies™, director of FamilyLife Blended® (a division of FamilyLife®), and the author/coauthor of numerous books including *The Smart Stepfamily Marriage*, *The Smart Stepmom*, *The Smart Stepdad*, *Dating and the Single Parent*, and the bestselling *The Smart Stepfamily*. In addition, he is the consulting editor of the SMART STEPFAMILY series and has published over a dozen videos and study resources, and hundreds of magazine and online articles. His work has been quoted/referenced by many news outlets such as the *New York Times*, the *Wall Street Journal*, and *USA Today*. Ron's books, conference events, social media presence, online resources, and one-minute radio feature *FamilyLife Blended* (heard daily on hundreds of stations nationwide and online) make him the leading voice on blended families in the US. He is a licensed marriage and family therapist who frequently appears in the national media, including *FamilyLife Today* and *Focus on the Family*, and he conducts marriage and family seminars around the country and internationally. He and his wife, Nan, have three boys. For more information, visit RonDeal.org, SmartStepfamilies.com, and FamilyLife.com

# More Vital Blended Family Resources from the Top Name in Stepfamily Ministry!

Visit smartstepfamilies.com and familylifeblended.com for additional information.

These 365 short and sweet thoughts, specifically for stepfamilies, will keep your family blending and bonding throughout the year. Each daily dose of encouragement includes a prayer for your home. Sharing these readings with your spouse and, when appropriate, kids will spark valuable conversations that foster family understanding and closeness.

*Daily Encouragement for the Smart Stepfamily* by Ron L. Deal with Dianne Neal Matthews

Stepfamily experts Ron L. Deal and Laura Petherbridge show you how to survive and thrive as a stepmom, including how to be a positive influence on the children and how to deal with conflict, as well as practical issues like dealing with holidays and between-home communication.

*The Smart Stepmom* by Ron L. Deal and Laura Petherbridge

Here is the survival guide every stepfather needs to succeed. Ron Deal equips stepdads everywhere with advice on everything—from how to connect with your stepchildren to handling tricky issues such as discipline and dealing with your wife's ex.

*The Smart Stepdad* by Ron L. Deal